How to Read and Write POETRY

How to Read and Write POETRY

Anna Cosman

FRANKLIN WATTS
NEW YORK • LONDON • 1979
A FIRST BOOK

LIBRARY OF CONGRESS CATALOGING IN PUBLICATION DATA
Cosman, Anna
How to read and write poetry.

(A First book)
Includes index.
SUMMARY: Discusses the reading and writing of
different forms of poetry. Includes examples of
works by Robert Frost and David Young.
1. Poetics—Juvenile literature. [1. Poetics] I. Title.
PN1042.C59   808.1   78-11861
ISBN 0-531-02261-7

Contents

ACKNOWLEDGMENTS

"Fast Isn't Far," "What Johnny Told Me," and "I Hate to Wait" by John Ciardi. From *Fast and Slow,* by John Ciardi. Copyright © 1975 by John Ciardi. Art by Becky Gaver. Reprinted by permission of Houghton Mifflin Company, publishers.

"Look, the Sea!" by William Zorach. From *Poetry,* Vol. XII, September 1918. Copyright © 1918 by The Modern Poetry Association. Reprinted by permission of the Editor of *Poetry.* Art by Adrienne Adams from *Poetry of Earth,* selected and illustrated by Adrienne Adams. Art copyright © 1972 by Adrienne Adams Anderson. Reprinted by permission of Charles Scribner's Sons, publishers.

"Dust of Snow," "Stopping by Woods on a Snowy Evening" and "Acquainted With the Night" by Robert Frost. From *The Poetry of Robert Frost,* edited by Edward Connery Lathem. Copyright 1923, 1928 © 1969 by Holt, Rinehart and Winston. Copyright 1951, © 1956 by Robert Frost. Reprinted by permission of Holt, Rinehart and Winston Publishers. Art by Adrienne Adams. From *Poetry of Earth,* selected and illustrated by Adrienne Adams. Art copyright © 1972 by Adrienne Adams Anderson. Reprinted by permission of Charles Scribner's Sons, publishers.

"The Sandhill Crane" by Mary Austin. From *The Children Sing in the Far West,* by Mary Austin. Copyright © 1928 by Mary Austin. Copyright renewed 1956 by Kenneth M. Chapman and Mary C. Wheelright. Reprinted by permission of the publisher, Houghton Mifflin Company. Art by Adrienne Adams. From *Poetry of Earth,* selected and illustrated by Adrienne Adams. Art copyright © 1972 by Adrienne Adams Anderson. Reprinted by permission of Charles Scribner's Sons, publishers.

"Egrets" by Judith Wright. From *The Double Tree* by Judith Wright. Copyright © 1978 by Judith Wright. Reprinted by permission of Houghton Mifflin Company and Angus & Robertson Publishers, Sydney. Art by Adrienne Adams from *Poetry of Earth,* selected and illustrated by Adrienne Adams. Art copyright © 1972 by Adrienne Adams Anderson. Reprinted by permission of Charles Scribner's Sons, publishers.

"White Butterflies" by Algernon Charles Swinburne. Art from *Poetry of Earth* selected and illustrated by Adrienne Adams. Art copyright © 1972 by Adrienne Adams Anderson. Reprinted by permission of Charles Scribner's Sons, publishers.

"Flower," "Rock," "Up and Down" and "Water" by Magnus Malmsten. Copyright © 1978 by Magnus Malmsten. World English language rights for use in this book granted by Magnus Malmsten. No further use of the material authorized without Mr. Malmsten's written permission.

"On the Beach" and "Dead Tree" by Robert Froman. From *Seeing Things: A Book of Poems* by Robert Froman. Lettering by Ray Barber. Copyright © 1974 by Robert Froman. Reprinted by permission of Thomas Y. Crowell, publishers.

"Forsythia" by Mary Ellen Solt. From *Concrete Poetry: A World View,* edited by Mary Ellen Solt. Copyright © 1968 by Indiana University Press. Reprinted by permission of Indiana University Press.

"Showers, Clearing Later in the Day" and "Landscape" by Eve Merriam. From *Finding a Poem* by Eve Merriam. Copyright © 1970 by Eve Merriam. Reprinted by permission of Eve Merriam, c/o International Creative Management. Art by Seymour Chwast. Reprinted by permission of Atheneum Publishers.

"Mother, may I go and swim?" from *A Great Big Ugly Man Came Up and Tied His Horse to Me: A Book of Nonsense Verse,* illustrated by Wallace Tripp (originally in color). Art copyright © 1973 by Wallace Tripp. Reprinted by permission of Little, Brown and Company, publishers.

"hist whist" by E. E. Cummings is reprinted from *Tulips & Chimneys* by E. E. Cummings, with the permission of Liveright Publishing Corporation. Copyright © 1923, 1925 and renewed 1951, 1953 by E. E. Cummings. Copyright © 1973, 1976 by Nancy T. Andrews. Copyright © 1973, 1976 by George James Firmage. Copyright © 1976 by Richard S. Kennedy. Art by Trina Schart Hyman. Copyright © 1976 by Trina Schart Hyman. From *Witch Poems.* Used by permission of Holiday House, Inc.

"Velvet Shoes" by Elinor Wylie. Copyright 1921 by Alfred A. Knopf, Inc. and renewed 1949 by William Rose Benet. Reprinted from *Collected Poems of Elinor Wylie,* by permission of Alfred A. Knopf, Inc., publishers. From *Poetry of Earth,* selected and illustrated by Adrienne Adams. Art copyright © 1972 by Adrienne Adams Anderson. Reprinted by permission of Charles Scribner's Sons, publishers.

"Poem for Wrists" by David Young. Copyright © 1973 by David Young. From *Boxcars,* published by The Ecco Press, and reprinted by permission.

Haiku poetry from *Japanese Haiku.* Copyright © 1955 by Peter Pauper Press, translated by Peter Beilenson.

How to
Read and Write
POETRY

For My Grandmothers
Helene Dalberg Cosman and Ida Pruitt

The Big Mac attack

The last time my friend TeeJay, who is eleven, came to visit me, he had a Big Mac attack.

> Get away! Get back!
> It's a Big Mac attack!
> Gimme a Big Mac real quick
> Or I'll crack!

He came up with those lines right in the middle of the street.

Later, while he was getting catsup on his shirt, I said to him: "I didn't know you were a poet, TeeJay."

"Yeah? Well, that makes two of us. I didn't know it either," he said.

"No — really — I thought your Big Mac attack was a poem," I told him.

"I thought it was just being silly. Do you really think that was a poem, Anna?"

"Yes. Because it expressed your feelings."

TeeJay ate for a minute, then said: "What if I had told you: 'I'm really hungry. Please get me a Big Mac.' That would be expressing my feelings, so that should be a poem, too." TeeJay is very logical.

I was stumped, so I asked for time to think. I thought while TeeJay slurped his strawberry milkshake. After a couple of minutes I said: "You were really hungry for your Big Mac, right? You wanted it a lot and you wanted it right away. You expressed that feeling through sound, rhythm, and rhyme. You exaggerated the feeling — made it larger than life — in order to make it real."

TeeJay nodded and said, "Yeah. Okay."

So I went on: "Remember how your poem was full of hard sounds: the 'k' sounds you ended the lines with? The hard 'g's' and the 'b's'? Those sounds have a snappy, brisk feeling. I could *hear* how hungry you were."

"Right. It wouldn't have worked if I had used long, droopy words."

"And you also used rhyme and rhythm to express the feeling of urgency. The first three lines ended with A-C-K. The last line ended with I-C-K. Those sounds are all hard, quick, and funny. Which is the feeling you were expressing."

"But I never thought about that," TeeJay argued. "The words just came out—"

"Which is why I think you are a poet. You ordered the sounds without knowing it."

TeeJay ate his French fries for a while in silence. I could tell he was thinking.

"Okay," he said, after a minute or two. "I get it, I think. All the sounds, and the beat and rhythm of the words, were funny and fast. Which is how I felt about wanting a Big Mac, really."

"Right. And you expressed that feeling through an image, too. You said you wanted your Big Mac so much you would *crack* if you didn't get it."

"Okay. I think I get it. A poem is making a feeling seem real all over again. Not just saying what a feeling is," TeeJay said.

"Right, TeeJay. You got it."

And we left to go to our favorite record store.

Poetry is...

A few days later, when I was listening to the record we had bought, I thought about TeeJay and our talk about his poem. I decided to see how M. L. Rosenthal, who taught me poetry in college, defined poetry. I got the book he wrote off my shelf and found this:

> Poetry is a human and personal activity. It is both expression and communication. It is a form of speech, and, while the raw material of poetry is experience, its medium is language. It is an ordering of words.

No wonder he's a famous critic and poet, I thought. That says it all. I wanted to be sure I understood what he was saying, so I outlined the paragraph.

1. **HUMAN AND PERSONAL ACTIVITY**
   Right. People write poems to say how they feel about something, to express an idea or thought. It's a personal activity because feelings are personal.

2. **EXPRESSION AND COMMUNICATION**
   Poetry is "expression" because it re-creates feelings and moods. It's "communication" because poetry clarifies thoughts and ideas.

3. **FORM OF SPEECH THAT TRANSFORMS EXPERIENCE INTO LANGUAGE**
   Experience gives us our feelings. Using words, poetry turns those feelings into poetry.

4. **IT IS AN ORDERING OF WORDS**
   Okay. We already know that poetry is experience turned into language. But that language — those words — need to be ordered. The words need to be put together to express the feeling and mood best.

All creative writing has the qualities Professor Rosenthal talks about. A good play, novel, or short story is a personal expression of a feeling drawn from experience. And the whole idea behind writing *anything* is to use words well. What really makes a poem a poem is the ordering of words.

Ordering words is something that we do every day. If you are writing a letter to someone special, you may write it two or three times before you like the way you put the

FAST ISN'T FAR

There was a boy with a souped-up car.
He drove it fast but not too far.
Just up to a curve he didn't quite make,
And through the fence, and into the lake.

Here's a poem by John Ciardi.
Do you hear how the rhyme helps
make the poem sound funny?

words together. If you have the time, you may write your English papers over a couple of times. (I never did, but I knew I was supposed to!)

Using words well in a letter means making sure you expressed your thoughts and feelings the best you could. When you reread it, you may decide to change a word or a sentence. It's the same thing when you do an English paper. You read it over and see that you should change some words. Maybe you should reorganize it, too. And you find that, as you keep ordering the words, your own thoughts and ideas become clearer.

ROBERT FROST'S POEM

Poetry works the same way. But the experience of poetry is different. Let's look at a poem by Robert Frost, one of America's best-loved and most famous poets. He read a poem at the inauguration of President John F. Kennedy. Robert Frost was a farmer who lived in New Hampshire. Many of his poems are about nature. This one is about his experience of night.

ACQUAINTED WITH THE NIGHT

I have been one acquainted with the night.
I have walked out in rain — and back in rain.
I have outwalked the furthest city light.

I have looked down the saddest city lane.
I have passed by the watchman on his beat
And dropped my eyes, unwilling to explain.

I have stood still and stopped the sound of feet
When far away an interrupted cry
Came over houses from another street,

But not to call me back or say good-bye;
And further still at an unearthly height
One luminary clock against the sky

Proclaimed the time was neither wrong nor right.
I have been one acquainted with the night.

Read through this poem once to yourself, and then read it out loud a few times. Listen to the way the poem sounds. Don't worry about understanding the poem at first. Just hear it.

Whenever you read a poem, it is very important to know exactly what each word means. This is because poets very often use words that have a number of meanings, and each meaning gives more depth to the poem. In this poem, there are a number of words that have a few meanings. "Acquainted" means to know something personally, to be informed about something, to be familiar with something. "Luminary" is an object in the sky, like the sun or the moon, that gives light. But "luminary" has another meaning, too: it is a source of light in the sense of understanding, of making something clear, either intellectually (through your mind) or spiritually. "Unearthly" means something beyond the earth, beyond natural things; something that is weird or impossible to explain. "Proclaim" is to announce publicly or officially, to make clear.

LOOK, THE SEA!
William Zorach

Look, the sea — how it lifts me in its arms like a child!
Oh, how I love to ride on the white foam of the waves
And dive down into the deep bottom of the sea!

Look, the sun — how it burns me like a leaf!
Oh, how I love to bathe in the hot rays of the sun
And burn like a flame in the sands!

Look, the moon — how it rides me in the sky!
Oh, how I love to sail on the shining edge of the clouds,
And sleep in the cool depths of the blue!

Each of these three stanzas is constructed in the same way. Do you see how the structure makes the idea of the poem easier to understand?

WHITE BUTTERFLIES
Algernon Charles Swinburne

Fly, white butterflies, out to sea,
Frail, pale wings for the wind to try,
Small white wings that we scarce can see,
       Fly!

Some fly light as a laugh of glee,
Some fly soft as a long, low sigh;
All to the haven where each would be,
       Fly!

How many stanzas in this poem? Two.
How many lines in each stanza? Four.

This poem is seven sentences long. Find where each sentence ends. But, in poetry, we don't talk about sentences; we talk about *lines*. A line of poetry is all the words that are printed on one line. The first line of this poem is one sentence. But the fifth and sixth lines together are a sentence.

A group of sentences that go together in most writing is called a paragraph. In poetry, a group of lines that go together is called a *stanza*. This poem is five stanzas long. It is also fourteen lines long.

Let's go through the stanzas together so we can be sure we understand what Robert Frost is saying in this poem. In the first stanza, he tells us that he knows the night, has gone for walks in the rain. But what kind of walks? For *long* walks, for he says he has "outwalked" the "furthest light in the city." Remember: in poetry, every word counts.

In the second stanza, he tells us what he has done on these walks: looked down streets, passed a watchman. But, he also gives us a feeling about what his walks have been like. "Saddest" is the word he uses to describe what he has seen. In the last line of the stanza, he says he looked down when he passed a watchman, "unwilling to explain." Explain *what?* That's a puzzling statement, isn't it? What do you think he means by that? Do you think he knows that there is no real reason for his walk, that he is just trying to get to know the night? Do you think that is something he could *explain* to the watchman?

When he stops walking, in stanza three, he stops the "sound of feet." He is alone in the night, isn't he? His are the only footsteps. But, using an image — a picture — to say that he is alone has more force than if he simply wrote: "I was alone." He hears a cry. In stanza four he tells us that the sound is not directed at him. I think that makes his loneliness more real. Do you?

He keeps walking and sees a clock high up against the sky. It is a *luminary* clock at an *unearthly* height. Take a look at the meanings of those two words again. Then reread the lines. The clock is lit, but it is lit the way the sun and moon are lit. It is high up in the air, but it is beyond the earth, beyond what is natural.

The last stanza is hard to understand, isn't it? How can time be "neither wrong nor right"? That doesn't make sense, does it? What do you think Robert Frost meant by that? When I think about that line, I can feel my brain working, but then the answer slips away.

Each time I read this poem, though, I feel a little closer to understanding that line. Do you think Frost's idea about time is something that only makes sense as part of the *experience* of this poem? Could this be a thought or idea that only "one acquainted with the night" could have?

Take a look at the poem again and notice that the first and last lines are exactly the same. The first time you read that line, you see it as a statement of fact, don't you? But what about the second time you read the line? Do you begin to see other meanings in the statement? That is because Robert Frost has re-created the experience of the night in his poem. We read the poem and go through the experience with him and slowly begin to understand what the night means to Robert Frost.

Look at the last word in each line. Make a list of all those words. Do you see the way Robert Frost has used

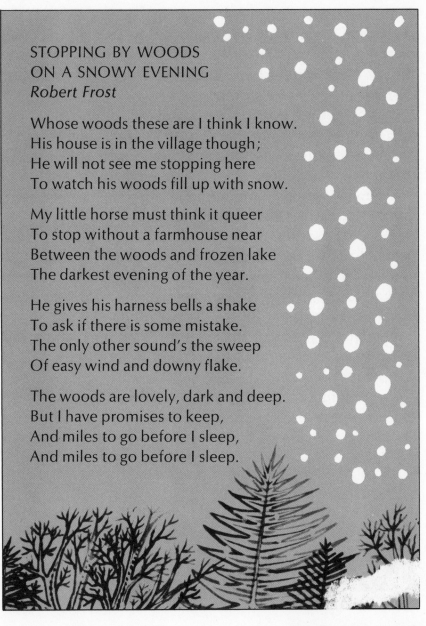

STOPPING BY WOODS
ON A SNOWY EVENING
Robert Frost

Whose woods these are I think I know.
His house is in the village though;
He will not see me stopping here
To watch his woods fill up with snow.

My little horse must think it queer
To stop without a farmhouse near
Between the woods and frozen lake
The darkest evening of the year.

He gives his harness bells a shake
To ask if there is some mistake.
The only other sound's the sweep
Of easy wind and downy flake.

The woods are lovely, dark and deep.
But I have promises to keep,
And miles to go before I sleep,
And miles to go before I sleep.

**Another poem by Robert Frost.
Read it three or four times; you'll
find more in it each time you do.**

rhyme? The first and third line of each stanza rhyme. And the second line provides the rhyme for the stanza that comes next. For example, in stanza one "night" rhymes with "light." And "rain" — the middle line — provides the rhyme for stanza two: "lane" and "explain."

Look at the length of the sentences in the poem. The first, second, third, and fourth lines are each one sentence long. But look how the sentences get longer. The sentence that starts stanza three doesn't end until the beginning of stanza five. The long sentence builds up speed in the poem: it makes one very long sound.

A poet uses rhyme and rhythm to help create the experience of the poem. A poem doesn't have to rhyme: it's up to the poet to decide whether or not it should. Robert Frost wanted to use rhyme. He decided that it would help make the night real to us.

Read this poem again tomorrow. And then read it in a week. Every time you read it, you will see more and more in it, because poems don't work the way most writing works. Remember that reading a poem is an *experience* and, each time you have the experience, it will be richer and more interesting for you.

Writing your first poem

We've seen how Robert Frost used words to express his feelings. Let's do the same thing ourselves: let's write our first poem. I thought you might like to write a poem about an animal. And I'll do one, too.

Pick an animal you have some feelings about. Maybe it's your pet. It could be the pack of stray cats that hang out in the street near your house. It could be the puppy you found but weren't allowed to keep. Take your time and pick your animal carefully: you'll know when you have the right one. I'm going to write about a cat, named Danny, I used to have.

When you see the animal, how do you see him? Does your dog or cat come into your mind as just a picture? Or is he doing something? If you relax, and let your mind go clear, you'll see your animal *doing* something. Just take your time.

Write down whatever it is you see him doing. Don't worry about getting the words right. Describe the picture quickly before you forget it. Then relax and take your time again, and think of another picture. Write that one down, too. And then do it one more time.

You now have three pictures of how you see your animal. These images will be the basis of your poem. Here are my pictures:

1. Danny chases his tail, running faster and faster around in a circle. Then—suddenly!—he sits down and starts CHEWING his tail.

2. Danny trips over his dish of milk, spills it, and looks around to see if anyone saw him. He sneaks away and falls asleep under the bed.

3. Danny runs into the living room very fast and stops suddenly for no reason. He stares straight ahead and then arches his back. But there isn't anything there at all: he's staring at nothing. After a while, he walks away as if nothing had happened.

I just wrote the pictures down. I didn't worry about getting the words right. When you've finished writing down your pictures, we can start to turn our words into poems.

The first thing we'll do is order the pictures. That's how we can start to structure our poems. The right order is the order that makes sense, that expresses your feelings best.

THE SANDHILL CRANE
Mary Austin

Whenever the days are cool and clear
The sandhill crane goes walking
Across the field by the flashing weir*
Slowly, solemnly stalking.
The little frogs in the tules* hear
And jump for their lives when he comes near,
The minnows* scuttle* away in fear,
When the sandhill crane goes walking.

The field folk know if he comes that way,
Slowly, solemnly stalking,
There is danger and death in the least delay
When the sandhill crane goes walking.
The chipmunks stop in the midst of their play,
The gophers hide in their hole away
And hush, oh, hush! the field mice say,
When the sandhill crane goes walking.

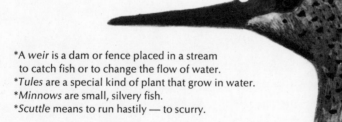

*A *weir* is a dam or fence placed in a stream
  to catch fish or to change the flow of water.
Tules are a special kind of plant that grow in water.
Minnows are small, silvery fish.
Scuttle means to run hastily — to scurry.

**Here's a poem about a bird.
I looked up the hard words for you.**

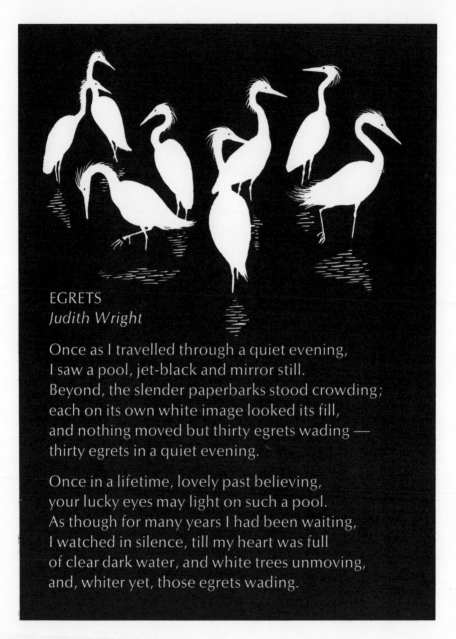

EGRETS
Judith Wright

Once as I travelled through a quiet evening,
I saw a pool, jet-black and mirror still.
Beyond, the slender paperbarks stood crowding;
each on its own white image looked its fill,
and nothing moved but thirty egrets wading —
thirty egrets in a quiet evening.

Once in a lifetime, lovely past believing,
your lucky eyes may light on such a pool.
As though for many years I had been waiting,
I watched in silence, till my heart was full
of clear dark water, and white trees unmoving,
and, whiter yet, those egrets wading.

**One of the ways that Judith Wright
recreates her experience for us
is through her use of adjectives.**

See the animal doing the three different things over and over. Just close your eyes, and, after a while, you'll see the pictures in the right order. When that happens, number your pictures.

Here's what I did. I thought about Danny and I saw him run into the room first. Then I saw him stare ahead, walk away. Next I saw him chase and chew his tail. The last thing I saw Danny do was spill his milk and go hide under the bed.

I think that order is the right one. It makes *sense* for Danny to charge into the room in the beginning of the poem and be asleep at the end. It is the order that expresses the feeling I get from Danny the best.

Once you have the right order for your poem, think about why it seems right. You will be able to write a better poem if you *know* why you have things in the order you have. The right order expresses your feelings best.

In my poem, Danny moves from being silly and crazy to being just a cat, asleep under the bed. See what your animal does. What does he start out as? How does he end up? Understand what happens in your poem. It will help you write it.

Read and think about what you have written. You'll see more and more ideas and feelings in your three pictures. You'll see what you really want to say in your poem and what you really feel about the animal. Write down all the thoughts that come into your head about your poem.

LET'S STOP IN THE MIDDLE
Our poems are more than half done now. We have figured out what we want to say and the order in which we want to

say it. Now we have to order our words to best express our feelings. Before we do that, I thought I'd show you a poem that a famous poet, Carl Sandburg, wrote about a dog.

> The old dog barks backwards without getting up.
> I can remember when he was a pup.

How do you feel when you read that poem? I feel sort of sorry for the old dog, but I feel good at the same time. Good because the man has had his dog for a long time.

I also think when I read this poem. I find myself thinking about the way time passes. I think about what it must be like to become older and see the changes in the world. I think about time and I think about death, too.

But none of those ideas are put down in words on the page, are they? The poet just wrote two lines of words — simple, everyday words — about a dog. But he used his words so well that he created a lot of feelings in very few words. How come?

Read the poem again. Do you see how very simple it is? The only adjective is "old." The only adverb is "backwards." But those two words create the strongest emotion, don't they? The feeling the poem creates is about being old and looking backwards.

Read the poem out loud and listen to the way the words sound. The poem has a slow, steady beat to it, doesn't it? The words come out in a way that expresses a slow, sad feeling. That's because Sandburg chose short words, for one thing. There's a slight rhyme here, too, although it slips by you. You don't really *hear* the rhyme.

Read this poem a few times. Think about it for a while. After you think you understand how it works, turn the page and then we can finish our poems.

FINISHING YOUR FIRST POEM

All we need to do now to finish our poems is to get the words in the right order. You saw how carefully and well Sandburg chose his words. How do we pick ours?

First, look at what you have written down. Read the thoughts you wrote down next to your pictures. Think carefully about what you are really trying to say. Remember that you are expressing your feelings in this poem: make sure you understand what they are.

Start reworking the words you already have. Keep reading, writing, reading and rewriting. You'll hear which words sound wrong. You'll know which words are right. You want to express your feelings: the right words sound like and define your feelings best.

This is your poem. You can change it any time you want to. Some poems take only a few minutes to write. Some poems take days and days. The next time you feel restless or unhappy, try writing a poem. You'll find there's a poem — and a feeling — waiting inside of you.

Let me show you the poem I wrote about Danny. I should first tell you that LEX AVE EXPRESS is short for the Lexington Avenue Express, which is a subway in New York City. (Always make sure you understand *every* word in a poem. I know it can be a drag to look things up in the dictionary, but you really should.)

Danny comes in on the LEX AVE EXPRESS
jumps off. Who's this!
He stares straight ahead.
Circling, circling, he catches that old rascal, tail.
Sits down for a good chew.
The train derails by the milk dish.
It's been a long day. Danny dreams under the bed.

I used the picture of Danny riding on a subway train to express the feeling of his speed. Do you see how I used it again in the sixth line? A picture that is developed in a poem is called an image.

Look at the fourth line. If you read it out loud, you can hear all the hard "c's" in the line. Do you hear the way those sounds build up the feeling of speed? The words "circling, circling" present an image of speed, too, don't they?

Now read the last two lines out loud. Listen to all the "d" sounds and the long "a" sounds. Do you hear the way that part of the poem slows down? I tried to use words that sound most like the feeling I was expressing.

A concrete poem!

There is a group of young poets today who are writing what they call "concrete" poetry. Concrete is not just cement; the word also means something that can be seen, something that is real, something that is physical. In order for something to be "concrete," it has to exist in space.

What these poets are doing is emphasizing the "experience" of poetry. Remember when we said that poetry is a form of speech that transforms experience into language? That is the third part of our definition of poetry. These poets are saying that they experience the language. They are saying that the words are the experience.

Take a look through the book. Those pages with just words on them are different concrete poems. In each of them, the word IS the experience.

Our first concrete poem
by Magnus Malmsten:
see the way the words
look like what they mean?

FLOWER FLOWER FLOWER FLOWER
FLOWER FLOWER FLOWER
FLOWER GRASS GRASS GRASS GRASS GRASS FLOWER GRASS GRASS
FLOWER GRASS GRASS GRASS GRASS LEAF FLOWER GRASS GRASS GRASS GRASS
GRASS GRASS FLOWER GRASS GRASS GRASS STONE LEAF GRASS
GRASS GRASS FLOWER LEAF GRASS GRASS STONE LEAF GRASS LEAF LEAF GRASS
GRASS LEAF STONE LEAF GRASS LEAF LEAF GRASS
LEAF LEAF LEAF LEAF LEAP

Rock rocks — right?
(Magnus Malmsten)

I think you'll find them interesting and fun to look at. They are not heavy, serious poems. In fact, some people say that this kind of poetry isn't really poetry.

What do you think? It's always good to ask people what their definition of art is. Don't ever let anyone tell you that something isn't art without getting them to explain why.

I think concrete poetry is poetry. And I think it would be fun to write a concrete poem with you. All you need to write a concrete poem is to see a word and to see the idea in the word at the same time. The concrete poem, "ROCK" rocks, doesn't it? The poem is doing what the word does. It's as simple as that. Just remember that your concrete poem has a whole page to itself. So it should fill that page.

Do you understand that? You know how a painting has to fill a whole canvas? It needs to fill the space it has been given. A concrete poem is like that, too. Since you are expressing just one idea on a whole page, make sure your idea can take up all that space.

To start our concrete poem is almost the same thing as writing it. Because, to start our poem, we need a word and an idea. And that's all the poem is.

Take any kind of word you want. You can use a verb, as the poet who wrote "ROCK" did. Or you can use a noun, an adverb, or whatever you want.

Once you have picked your word, see the word doing what it says. If this sounds confusing, just take a look through the book at the concrete poems. See what the poet did. And then you'll understand what you have to do. Just remember, your idea should be big and clever enough to fill a page.

Working with opposites,
Magnus Malmsten has
come up with an imaginative,
amusing concrete poem.

UP AND DOWN UP AND ~~DOWN~~ UP AND DOWN
UP AND DOWN UP AND DOWN UP AND DOWN
UP AND DOWN UP AND DOWN UP AND DOWN
UP AND DOWN UP AND DOWN UP AND DOWN
UP AND DOWN UP AND DOWN UP AND DOWN
UP AND DOWN UP AND DOWN UP AND DOWN
UP AND DOWN UP AND DOWN UP AND DOWN
UP AND DOWN UP AND DOWN UP AND DOWN
UP AND DOWN UP AND DOWN UP AND DOWN
UP AND DOWN UP AND DOWN UP AND DOWN
UP AND DOWN UP AND DOWN UP AND DOWN

**Left: Robert Froman found a
concrete poem at the beach.
Where can you find one?**

**Below: this poem is about
water, too, but the feeling
is calm and peaceful.
How do you see water?
(Magnus Malmsten)**

WATER WATER WATER
WATER WATER WATER WATER
TER WATER WATER WATER WATER WATER WATER
WATER WATER WATER WATER WATER WATER WATER WATER WAT
WATER WATER WATER WATER WATER WATER WATER WA
WATER WATER WATER WATER WATER WATER WATER WATER WATE
WATER WATER WATER WATER

This is the most fun of any kind of poetry to write. Because it's a kind of instant poetry. So, after you have written one concrete poem, try another.

Concrete poetry is a good kind of poetry to write and to read because it makes you stop and look at words. It makes you think about words. And a poem is just a group of words, isn't it?

The more words you know, the better you will be at writing poems. A good thing to do is to look up every word you come across that you don't understand. Keep a little notebook of new words. Read the dictionary. It sounds like it might be boring to do that, but it really isn't. It's one of the best things to do to become a better poet.

Two haiku

Another kind of poetry that I think you would enjoy writing is called haiku. You say it: HI-ku. Haiku is a type of poem that was developed in Japan five hundred years ago. But people in Japan still write haiku. Poets here write them, too, because they're fun to write. They're a kind of puzzle: there are special rules for writing them.

Haiku are written about nature — usually about one of the four seasons. They re-create the feeling of a season in sound and in images. The special rules are these: haiku must be three lines long. The first line has five *syllables*, the second line has seven syllables, and the third line has five syllables. (A syllable is a unit of the spoken word. "Cat" is one sound, so it is one syllable. "Syllable" is said "syl" "a"

"ble" — which is three units of sound — so it is three syllables.)

Let's take a look at two haiku and see how they are put
together.

> Hi! My little hut
> Is newly thatched I see . . .
> Blue morning glories.

> Yellow evening sun . . .
> The shadow of the scarecrow
> Reaches to the road.

Read through each of these a few times. Don't worry about
understanding them. Read them out loud. Do you hear the
way the syllables work? You might want to go through and
count out the five syllables in the first line, the seven in the
second, and the five syllables in the last. Let's go through
each of these haiku together.

The first haiku was written by a Japanese poet named
Kobayashi Issa who lived from 1763 to 1827. It was translated into English by an American, Peter Beilenson. It will
help you understand this haiku if you know that morning
glories are small, bright blue flowers that grow on a vine.
"Thatched" describes a kind of roof made from straw. To
"thatch" a roof is to put fresh straw on it to keep it strong.
Issa took the idea of thatching a roof and combined it with
the image of the flowers that blossomed on the roof. This is
a little hard to see and understand, but think about it until
you get the image.

Make sure you turn this poem by Mary Ellen Solt
on its side. You'll find a hidden message coming
out of FORSYTHIA. Do you know that forsythia
is a shrub that has tall, skinny, yellow spring flowers?

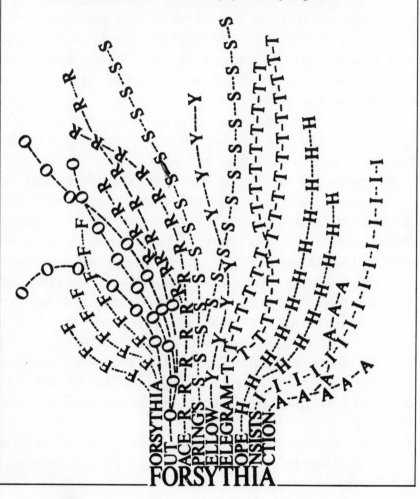

FORSYTHIA

Do you notice that the image comes together in the last line? Haiku works like that. You know how on TV you first see a general picture and then the camera moves in on a detail? Say you're watching a detective show. First, the detective comes into the room, and the camera shows you the whole room. But then, as he notices something, the camera moves in on the detail. Haiku works in the same way. First you see the general picture — in this haiku, you see the roof — and then you see the detail. Here, it's the morning glories.

On TV, the detail is often an important part of the story. The detective finds a clue and then puts together what he thinks happened. In haiku, the detail is an important part of the image and the feeling. The detail actually *creates* the feeling. In this haiku, the last line creates the surprise. We go from the image of the hut to the picture of its being "newly thatched" with flowers. That picture gives us the wonderful, sudden feeling of spring, doesn't it? You know how spring comes all at once: one day it is still cold and gray, but the next day you see some crocuses in bloom, or you notice a hedge has turned green. It is just that feeling of surprise and freshness that the haiku re-creates. In the first line, we are just looking at a hut. In the second line, we get a sense of something new beginning. In the last line, with just one image, the whole picture and feeling come together.

Take another look at the first haiku. Do you get the feeling of spring by reading it? Do you find that it re-creates that feeling for you? Now, read through the second haiku, and we can go through that one together.

This one was written by a man named Kuroyanagi Shoha and was also translated by Peter Beilenson. Shoha wrote during the Edo Period, which lasted from 1603 to 1868. It creates a very different feeling from the first one. First, we see the sun. But it's a special kind of sun: "yellow, evening" sun.

In the second line, we move from the sun to the shadow of the scarecrow. That image gives us that kind of sad feeling a fall night gives us. For one thing, in that line the poet takes us from the sun to the shadow. And we see the picture of the scarecrow.

In the last line, we see the shadow completely. We sense that darkness is moving in. We know that it is evening, but we also have the sad, lonesome feeling we get in the fall. We know that winter is coming. We have moved from the sun, which represents summer and light, to the shadow, which represents winter and darkness.

Read through the second haiku again. Do you see the way the picture we see becomes smaller and sharper? The way the three lines move to the detail? And the way the detail contains the surprise and creates the feeling of fall?

Writing haiku

I thought you might like to write a haiku of your own. You already know that haiku are always written about one of the four seasons, so pick one you'd like to write about. Maybe you want to write about the summer, and the way you feel when you go to the park. Maybe you love to go fishing in the spring and would like to tell about that feeling. First, decide which season to write about, and then think about why you like that season so much. Remember that haiku is about *nature*, so think about a feeling of nature you get from the season.

I'll write one with you. Remember when we wrote our poems about pets? The pictures just came into your mind, didn't they, after you relaxed. We'll do the same thing to write our haiku. Once you have decided what season you want to write about, relax and let your mind go clear. Don't think about anything, so that the picture will just be able to float into your mind.

When the picture comes into your mind, look at it carefully. Maybe what you see is a snowfall. From that picture you will want a detail for your last line. You know the way one snowflake will melt into the others that have already fallen? That picture of the single flake melting might be a good picture for the last line of a haiku about winter.

If I were going to write about fall, I might use the picture of apples falling off a tree, lying on the ground, and turning mushy. I think that image describes the feeling of fall. In the fall, everything goes back to the earth until the spring. The picture of a falling leaf works in the same way.

But I think I'll write a haiku about spring. And the image I want to focus on in the last line is a bird in the sun. Once you have decided on what you want your haiku to describe, decide what you want in the last line. Pick the detail your haiku moves toward first. Once you have your last line, let's go back and write the first two.

I told you my last line will be about a bird, sitting in the sun, at my window. I want to give the feeling of spring just arriving. So in my first two lines, I want to set the general picture. And I also want the last line to be a surprise. So the first two lines should form a contrast to the last one.

I think what I'll do to set up a contrast in my last line will be to describe a cold, gray winter day in the first two lines. After you have decided what you want your first two lines to describe, write that down.

SHOWERS, CLEARING LATER IN THE DAY

```
    !! !! !!    ! !     !
  !!!!!!!! !!!!  !! !!!
  !!!!!!!!!!!!!!!!!!!!!!!!
  !!!!!!!!!!!!!!!!!!!!!!!!
  !!!!!!!!!!!!!!!!!!!!!!!!!!          !!!!!
     !!!!!!!! !!!!!!!!!!!
   **!!!!!!!!!!
    .
        !! ! !!
     * ! * !         ⅄
     .    .
               ..   *  ! ! ...
                    .
              *
              .  ..

                   .



                                .




          *
          .
```

Eve Merriam has done it!
She's written a poem without any words!   •

Now you have your pictures. Let's go back and look at the two haiku in the book. Read them through, and you'll see that there are no extra words. That's because the poets had to keep in mind the number of syllables each line can have. Five in the first, seven in the second, and five in the last line. That special rule is what makes writing haiku different from writing other kinds of poetry. And that rule is what makes writing haiku fun, too.

So, take three pieces of paper. On the first one, write down the most general picture. Maybe it's a snowy field, or a stream in the summer. Remember the hut and the sun in the two haiku you've read. They are the most general images in those two poems. The first image tells us generally what you are looking at and thinking about.

Now, look at the most important detail in your image. What makes it special to you? What part of the picture best expresses your feeling about the season? Write that down on your second piece of paper. This image is the one your haiku will end on.

Now you have to figure out how you got from the general picture to the special one. Look at the two haiku we talked about. In the one about spring, we move from the hut to the morning glories. It is the middle line — the newly *thatched* hut — that gets us to the last line. That picture is the bridge between the two images. How did you get from the first line to the last? Think about that. When you think you understand what you did, write down that picture on the last piece of paper.

Okay? Now all you have to do is go back to these three pictures and put each of the images into the right number of syllables. On your first piece of paper, keep rewriting your picture until you can describe it in five syllables. It will take some time, so don't try to hurry. I'll show you what I did with my first line.

On my first piece of paper, I wrote: "A cold, gray, winter morning." But, when I had my poem figured out, I realized I couldn't say "gray" because the sun comes out in the last line. So, I decided to use the word "bleak." "Bleak" means hopeless. And I knew I would never have enough syllables to use the word "winter" because that would take up two of my five syllables. So I changed the word "winter" to "March." And March describes the season better. So, in five syllables I got: "A bleak March morning."

Once you have your first line done, you can start your second. Remember that in your second line you want to make a bridge to your third. In my second line, after playing around with the number of syllables, I got: "looks cold. A sudden sparrow . . ." I went from the cold March morning — the general picture — to the bird. Do the same thing in your second line. Remember that you can use a word like "Oh!" or "look!" for your syllable count if you want to.

If you get stuck working on your syllable count, just leave your haiku for a while. When you least expect it, the right words will just come to you. Don't get upset if this takes you a little while.

But, when you do get it right, turn to your last line. It's here that your detail will be the most focused. It's here that you will create the feeling of your season. For my last line I got: "suns in my window."

Inspired by trees,
Robert Froman
wrote this poem.

YOU LIVED A LONG TIME TREE. NOW YOU STAND AWHILE, BARE AND ALONE, A MON-UMENT TO YOUR PAST, UNTIL YOU ARE READY TO FALL AND BE-COME FOOD FOR YOUR FUTURE.

LANDSCAPE

What will you find at the edge of the world?
A footprint,
a feather,
desert sand swirled?
A tree of ice,
a rain of stars,
or a junkyard of cars?

What will there be at the rim of the earth?
A mollusc,*
a mammal,
a new creature's birth?
Eternal sunrise,
immortal sleep,
or cars piled up in a rusty heap?

Mollusc: a shellfish.

See how Eve Merriam set up her poem?
Compare stanzas one and two line by line.

I thought I'd show you how my haiku looks when it's all put together:

A bleak March morning
looks cold. A sudden sparrow
suns in my window.

Notice how the picture becomes clearer and clearer? Notice the way the last line is a surprise? Notice the syllable count? Now look at your haiku. Does your poem start with a general picture and move to a special one? Are you pleased with the way your haiku creates the feeling of the season you picked? Are your syllables right? Yes? Great! You just wrote a haiku.

A poem about wrists?

Some people think that poetry has to be about something important. When they think about poetry, they think about a great idea or a great emotion. But you can write a poem about anything.

And some people have their own ideas about what a poem should do. They might think it has to rhyme, for instance. Or that it has to be serious. Or that it has to be full of long, fancy words. Maybe they feel it should have a certain beat to it. Everyone has their own idea about what a poem should be like. Just remember that, once you have had some practice writing poetry, you can write your poems any way you want to.

I thought we'd take a look at a poem written by David P. Young. He teaches English at Oberlin College in Ohio. He

WHAT JOHNNY TOLD ME

I went to play with Billy. He
Threw my cap into a tree.
I threw his glasses in the ditch.
He dipped my shirt in a bucket of pitch.
I hid his shoes in the garbage can.
And then we heard the ice cream man.
So I bought him a cone. He bought me one.
A true good friend is a lot of fun!

**In poetry, you can be as silly as you want.
Here are two poems by
John Ciardi, guaranteed to make you grin.**

I HATE TO WAIT

Someone came to see me when I was not at home.
I let him in and told him I was sorry he had come
On just exactly almost the day I wasn't there.
So we made an appointment to meet again somewhere.
I think we said last Tuesday noon at quarter after eight.
He said he'd be there on the dot but that he might be late.
I said if he was there on time I would be glad to wait.
I even told my mother I was going to meet him there.
But now it's Thursday morning and I can't remember
  where
I was supposed to meet him. I know he hasn't come.
I'll give him ten more minutes. And then I'm going home.

has won lots of prizes for his poetry. I think this poem is interesting because it breaks a lot of rules that some people
have about the way a poem should be. Here's his poem:

POEM FOR WRISTS

Wrists! I want to
write you a poem you
whom nurses finger watches
circle razors open
handcuffs chill — you are
taken for granted wrists!
therefore assert yourselves
take charge of your
unruly friends the hands
keep them from triggers, off
necks give them a light
touch have them wave bye-bye
teach them to let
go at the right moment oh
wrists shy ankles of the arm
on whom farms flyrods
shovels whips and poems
so naturally depend.

When you first look at this poem, you will probably find it
very surprising. You may find it very hard to read. There is no
punctuation, no capitalization. There are none of the things
that we usually use to put words into order. In fact, it may
seem to you that there is no order in this poem at all.

But Mr. Young has come up with his own way of ordering words. He decided that he didn't want to use the regular rules when he wrote his poem. I thought what we could do would be to order this poem — to turn it into sentences — so that we could understand it. I have gone through and put this poem into sentences. Here's what I came up with:

Wrists! I want to write you a poem.
You, whom nurses finger, watches circle, razors open,
    handcuffs chill.
You are taken for granted, wrists!
Therefore: assert yourselves.
Take charge of your unruly friends, the hands.
Keep them from triggers, off necks.
Give them a light touch.
Have them wave bye-bye.
Teach them to let go at the right moment.
Oh, wrists. Shy ankles of the arm.
On whom farms, flyrods, shovels, whips, and poems so
    naturally depend.

Read through this a couple of times. I think you will start to understand the poem. Then go back and read it the way Mr. Young wrote his poem. Do you hear a certain funny, crazy beat when you read his poem out loud? Don't worry about understanding the whole poem right now. Just experience the words the way Young wrote them down.

I know this isn't an easy poem to understand. After you have read it out loud and heard it, let's go through and see what Young is really saying here.

Mother, may I go and swim?
Yes, my darling daughter.
Hang your clothes on yonder limb,
But don't go near the water.

**Something just for fun
before we go on.**

Yes.
A poem about
wrists.

Young tells us in the first line what he wants to do: he wants to write a poem to wrists. At first, that may seem like a pretty silly idea. But he tells the wrists *why* he wants to write them a poem. He tells wrists he appreciates what they have to go through. When a nurse takes your pulse, she uses wrists to do it. That's what he means by "whom nurses finger." A watch "circles" a wrist. "Razors open" isn't that easy to understand. Some people kill themselves by cutting open the veins in their wrists. "Handcuffs chill" describes what wrists have to go through if you get arrested. Wrists have to put up with and go through a lot if you stop to think about it. But they are "taken for granted." No one ever *does* stop to think about them.

So Young tells wrists to "assert themselves." That means

that they should be more forceful, more aggressive. And he also tells them they should "take charge of your unruly friends, the hands." "Unruly" means something that is hard to control, hard to manage. And he gives a list of things that hands have to be kept away from.

This list looks as disorganized as the first list Young gave us. But, if you go through it word by word, you'll see what he is talking about. Hands have to learn not to be violent. They have to be kept away from the triggers on guns. They have to be kept off the necks of people: in other words, they have to stop strangling! Hands need to learn a "light touch." They need to learn to say good-bye. They need to learn to let go at the right moment.

When he gave the list of things that wrists do at the beginning of the poem, Young went through a large variety of images. He does the same thing in this part of the poem. Do you notice that he goes from the most violent and extreme image — pulling a trigger on a gun — to the gentlest one — letting go? He is always changing the kind of image he uses. With almost every word, he has painted a new picture.

After he tells wrists what they should be doing, he goes back to telling them how great they are. He calls them "shy ankles of the arm." Do you understand that image? A wrist is to the arm what an ankle is to the leg. And then Young ends his poem with a list of things that wouldn't be possible without wrists. Again: look at the great variety of things he mentions: from farms to flyrods, which are a kind of fishing pole, in just two words. And he ends by saying that even poems wouldn't be possible without wrists.

Now that you understand the poem, go back and read it again. Do you see that the feeling the poem creates works much better the way Mr. Young wrote his poem than the way I rewrote it? By making up his own rules, he created a very special, fast-paced kind of crazy poem. He wanted the words to come out very fast, one right on top of the other. So that's what he did. If he had stopped the words with punctuation, we wouldn't get the same feeling from the poem.

After you have read the poem a few times, do you begin to sense that Young is writing about something more than wrists? I think he is really writing about the need to control violence, too. He sets up two opposite forces in his poem. He is writing about the "shy" wrists vs. the "unruly" hands, isn't he? And those two opposite forces contain the idea that there needs to be control on our violent impulses and on our anger. Hands are described as being angry and violent, while wrists are shown to be good and gentle. Hands pull triggers. Wrists make farms grow. Write poems.

Mr. Young took a very simple thing, a thing we never stop to think about, and made us look at it. He also drew on many ideas in the way he showed us that simple thing. He decided that there was a lot more to wrists than most people realized. And then he told us what he saw in wrists.

Each time you read his poem, I think you'll find something else to think about. You can just enjoy it as a kind of crazy poem about wrists, or you can dig deeper into it. Remember that the more times you read a poem, the more you'll see in it.

HIST WHIST

hist   whist
little ghostthings
tip-toe
twinkle-toe

little twitchy
witches and tingling
goblins
hob-a-nob   hob-a-nob

little hoppy happy
toad in tweeds
tweeds
little itchy mousies

with scuttling
eyes   rustle and run   and
hidehidehide
whisk

whisk   look out for the old woman
with the wart on her nose
what she'll do to yer
nobody knows

for she knows the devil   ooch
the devil   ouch
the devil
ach   the great

green
dancing
devil
devil

devil
devil

    wheeEEE

**This poem by e. e. cummings is even better
when it's read out loud. Why not practice it a
few times and then go read it to someone?**

Poems are everywhere!

What David Young did was to see a poem in an unusual place. He saw a poem in wrists. He saw the poem because he really stopped to look at wrists.

That's one of the advantages to writing poetry. It helps you see things in a new way. Poetry makes you look at things you might not stop to look at otherwise. It makes you think about things you wouldn't stop to think about. That's why it's interesting to read poetry. And interesting to write it.

You can write a poem about anything. But you can only write a poem about anything if you are seeing that thing in a new way. It is the *process* of seeing that thing in a different way that gives us poetry. It is the *experience* of seeing something in a new way that is poetry.

For example, if you look at a watch, you see the face of the watch, the hands, the numbers on the face. Maybe you notice the band. But until you stop and think about what a watch represents, it remains a watch. Once you think about what a watch is, though, once you start to look beyond the physical presence of a watch, you see the watch as a symbol for time. You see an idea in the object. You see something abstract (a thought about time) in something real (the watch).

How do we go about seeing that? It seems so abstract, so vague, doesn't it? But isn't that what we have been doing all along?

We stopped to look at an animal. Really thought about that animal. And then we wrote about what we saw there.

When we wrote concrete poetry, we did the same thing. We stopped to really look at and think about a word. We saw the idea in a word. And then we turned that idea about a word into a poem.

We stopped to look at one of the four seasons. We saw a picture of the season, and then focused on one part of it. And, by using fancy rules, we turned that idea into a haiku.

Poetry is a way of looking at the world. It is a new way of seeing. And of turning your vision into words.

DUST OF SNOW
Robert Frost

The way a crow
Shook down on me
The dust of snow
From a hemlock tree

Has given my heart
A change of mood
And saved some part
Of a day I had rued.*

Rued means to feel sorry about,
to regret, to wish undone.

Our last Robert Frost poem:
take the time to read it slowly.

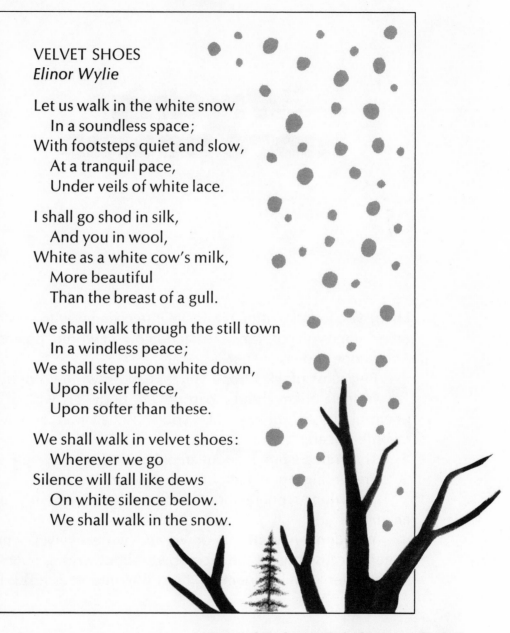

VELVET SHOES
Elinor Wylie

Let us walk in the white snow
  In a soundless space;
With footsteps quiet and slow,
  At a tranquil pace,
  Under veils of white lace.

I shall go shod in silk,
  And you in wool,
White as a white cow's milk,
  More beautiful
  Than the breast of a gull.

We shall walk through the still town
  In a windless peace;
We shall step upon white down,
  Upon silver fleece,
  Upon softer than these.

We shall walk in velvet shoes:
  Wherever we go
Silence will fall like dews
  On white silence below.
  We shall walk in the snow.

**Do you hear how quietly this poem rhymes?
The way the poem sounds
emphasizes the hushed feeling of a snowfall.**

Writing more poems

I hope you found writing poetry an interesting way to spend time. I hope you got some satisfaction out of writing poems. And I hope you enjoyed it.

But, most of all, I hope you'll keep on writing poetry. Try writing a poem about a part of your body. Try writing a poem about an object — like your baseball mitt or your favorite sweater.

Try writing a poem about an old person.

Try writing a poem about your mother.

Try writing a poem about your best friend. About your enemy.

You don't have to sit down and write every poem, either. Because one of the nicest parts about writing poems is that, after a while, poems will just pop into your head. It could be while you're taking a shower. It could be as you're walking home from school. Suddenly, when you least expect it, you'll hear some words start to form in the back of your head. When that happens, write down what you hear before you forget it. It could be a poem that is already finished. It could be a poem that needs a little work.

Get yourself a little notebook that is just for your poetry. Next time you see something in a new way, or you notice a detail that you keep thinking about, write it in your book. Then, when you feel like writing a poem, you'll have some ideas to work with.

You already know that it takes some work to write a poem. But don't turn it into a chore. Remember that you do not have to finish every poem that you start. You don't have to turn every idea you have about a poem into a poem, either. But, when you are in the mood, I hope you do spend a little time on your poems.

Poems make great presents. Give one to your mom for her next birthday. Write one to your father for Father's Day. I bet it will be one of the best presents you ever give.

Send a poem to a friend who is sick. Send a poem to your grandma.

It's good to give poems to other people. But the best thing about writing poems is how it makes *you* feel. Remember when I told you that, if you feel down or depressed, you should try writing a poem? It's true: you will get so involved in writing your poem that you'll forget about feeling blue. And as you write your poem, you'll begin to understand your feelings better.

There's one last thing: writing poetry can get lonely. Sometimes what you write won't make sense to anyone but you. Sometimes it won't even make much sense to you! It can be hard to find someone to share your poems with.

If you ever feel like sharing one of your poems with me, just send it to me. You can write to me at Franklin Watts, the people who published this book. Here is the address:

Anna Cosman
c/o Franklin Watts
730 Fifth Avenue
New York, N.Y. 10019

I hope to hear from you.

Index

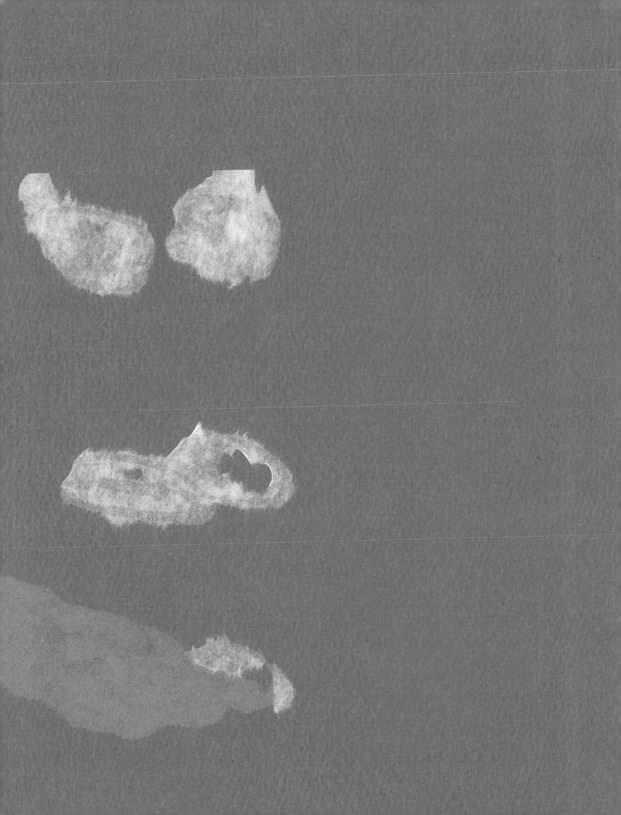